Activity Book

My Little Island
3

PEARSON

ALWAYS LEARNING

Pearson Education Limited
Edinburgh Gate
Harlow
Essex CM20 2JE
England
and Associated Companies throughout the world.

www.pearsonelt.com

© Pearson Education Limited 2012

The moral rights of the author have been asserted.

All rights reserved; no part of this publication may be reproduced, stored in a retrieval system, or transmitted in any form or by any means, electronic, mechanical, photocopying, recording, or otherwise without the prior written permission of the Publishers.

First published 2012
Twelfth impression 2021

ISBN: 978-1-4479-1361-0

Set in Fiendstar

Printed in Slovakia by Neografia

Illustrated by José Luis Briseño

Contents

1. Welcome 4
2. At School 14
3. Workers 22
4. My Town 32
5. Clothes 40
6. Feelings 50
7. Healthy Food 58
8. The Zoo 68
9. Places 76

Phonics 86
Certificate 94
Cutouts 95

1 Welcome

1 Trace. Draw candles and colour.

REVIEW

2 Count the shapes. Write and say. Colour.

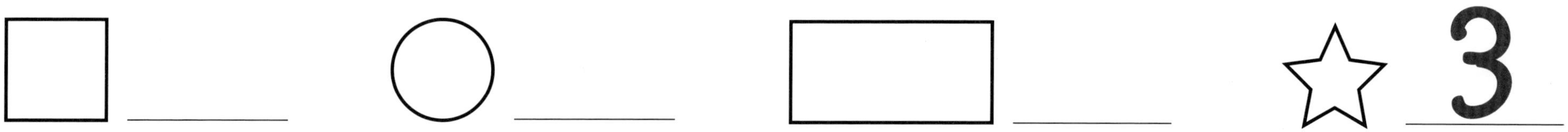

 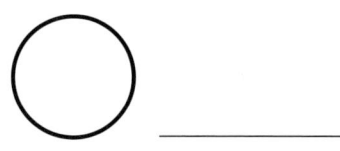 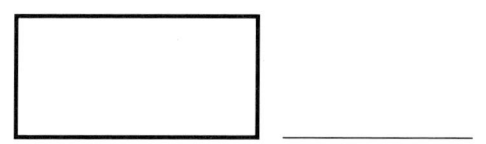  3

Practice: counting 1–5, shapes, toys, *It's a (square)*.

3 **What's missing in Picture B? Draw, colour, and say.**

A

B

Practice: classroom objects

4 Match, colour, and say.

Practice: toys

REVIEW

5 Match and draw. Colour and say.

Practice: family members

REVIEW

6 Draw what's missing. Colour and name the rooms.

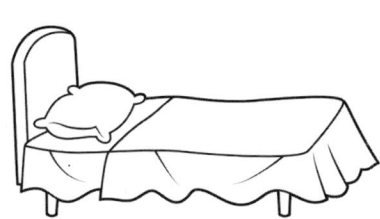  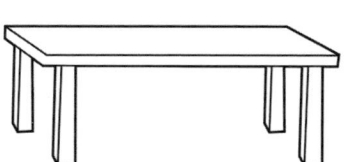 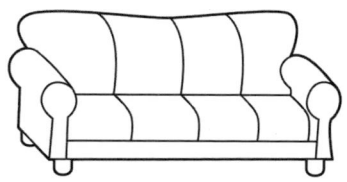

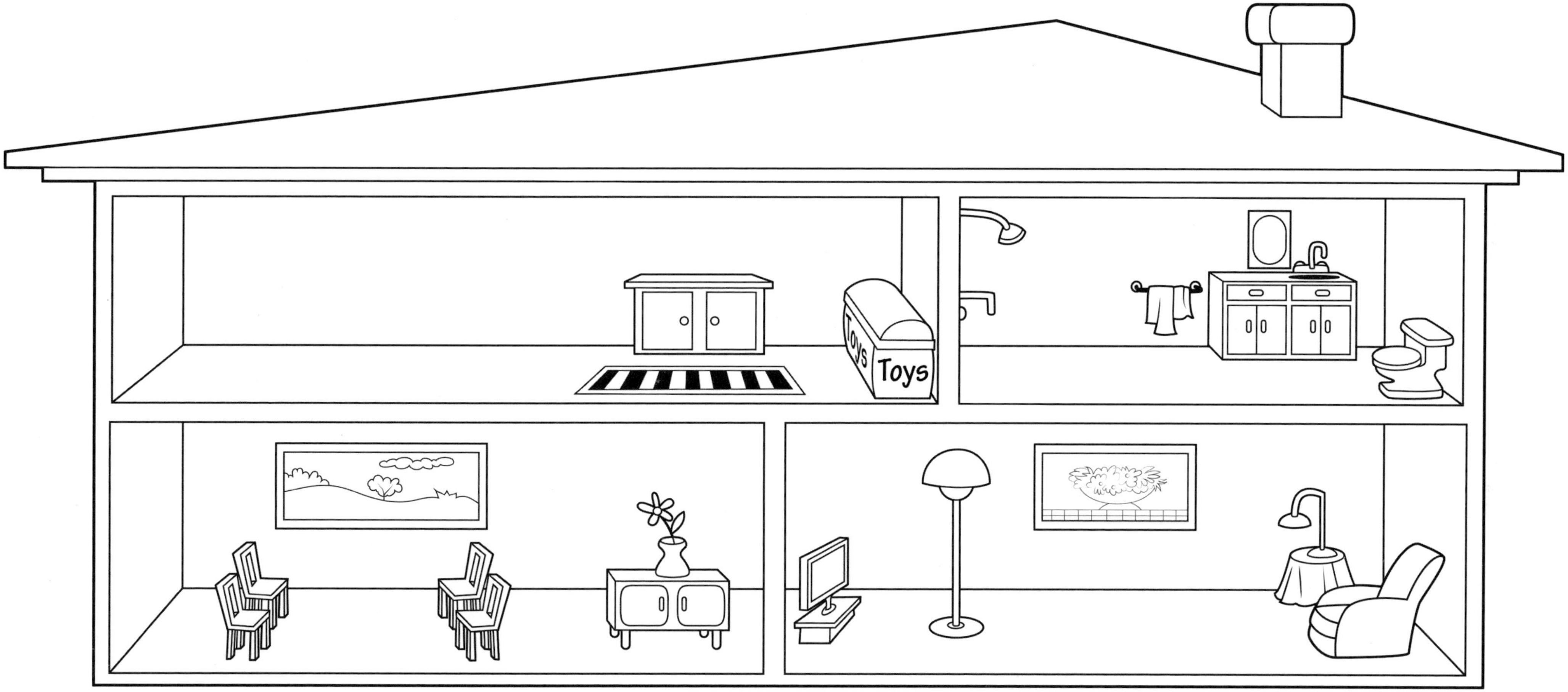

Practice: rooms

UNIT 1

REVIEW

7 Match, colour, and say.

Practice: food items

REVIEW

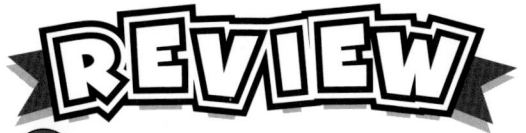

8 **Trace, colour, and say.**

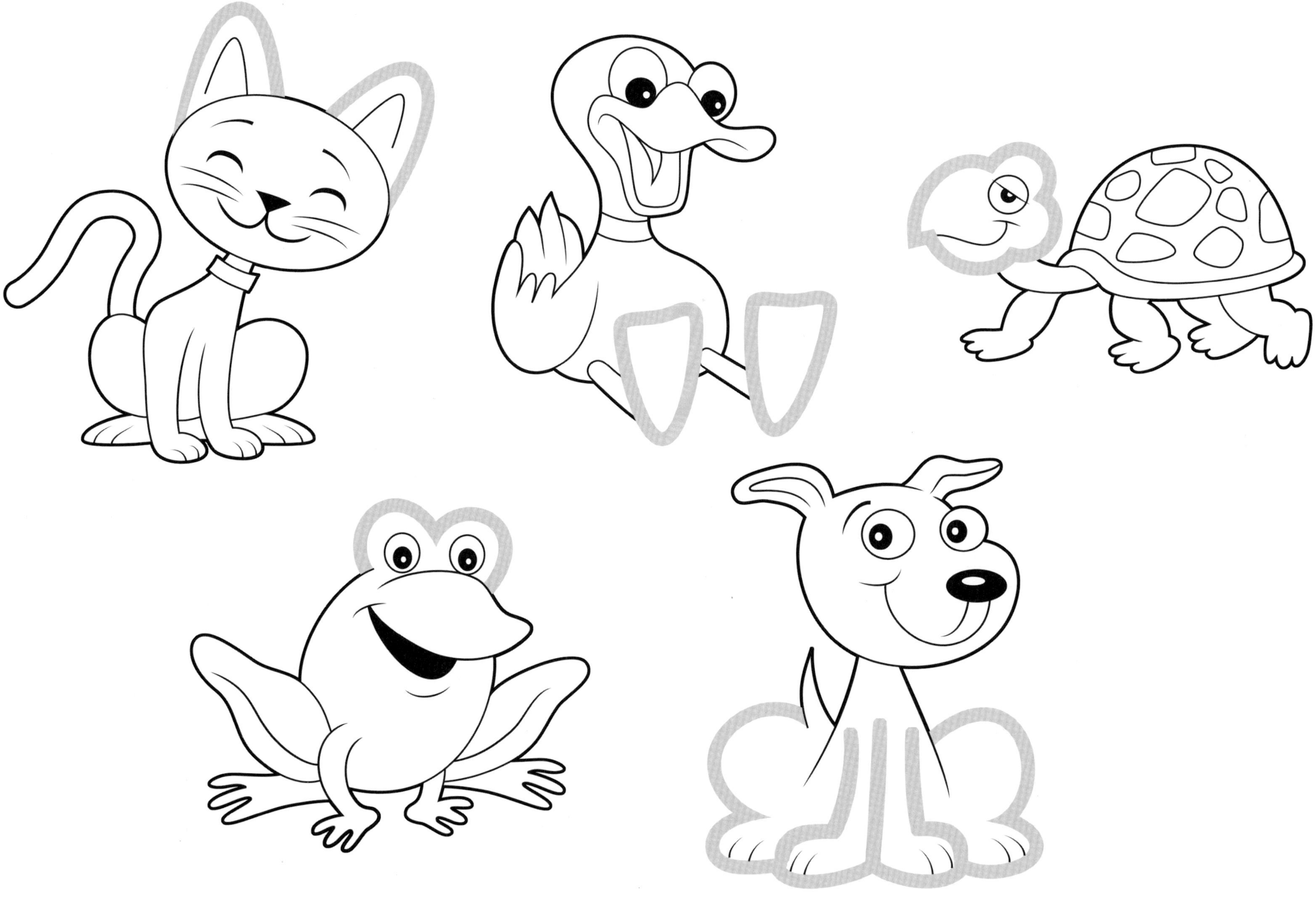

Practice: body parts, animals

REVIEW

9 Join the dots. Colour and say.

Practice: weather

10 Match and colour. Say.

p   t   l   s   m

Practice: initial letters and sounds

2 At School

1 Look and number. Colour and say.

  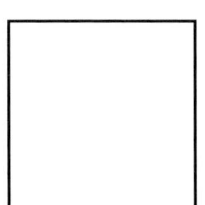 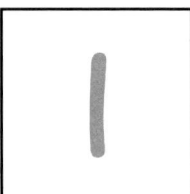

Practice: *classroom, computer room, music room, play, playground, read, sing, use the computer*

VOCABULARY

2 Match, colour, and say.

Practice: *classroom, computer room, music room, play, playground, read, sing, use the computer*

STORY PRACTICE

3 Trace the path. Ask and answer. Colour.

Practice: *Where do you (read)? In the (classroom).*

STORY PRACTICE

4 What is not in a music room? Circle and say. Colour.

UNIT 2

Practice: school vocabulary

SPEAKING

5 Spin a pencil. Ask and answer. Colour.

Practice: *Where do you (play)? In the (playground).*

SPEAKING

6 Ask and answer. Circle and colour.

Practice: *Where do you (sing)? In the (music room).*

UNIT 2

7 **Trace, count, and match. Colour and say.**

1 2 3 4 5

6 7 8 9 10

Practice: counting 1–10 Review: book, crayon, pencil

3 Workers

1 Join the dots. Colour and say.

Practice: *firefighter*

VOCABULARY

2 Match, colour, and say.

Practice: *artist, dentist, doctor, police officer* **Review:** *teacher*

STORY PRACTICE

3 **Circle what Sue wants to be in the story. Colour and say.**

Practice: *I want to be a (police officer).*

STORY PRACTICE

4 Trace, colour, and say.

Practice: *I want to be a (firefighter).*

5 Trace, colour, and say.

I want to be a police officer!

Practice: *I want to be a (police officer).*

SPEAKING

6 Trace and colour. Ask and answer.

Practice: *What do you want to be? I want to be a (doctor).*

UNIT 3

7 Trace, count, and write. Colour and say.

9   10   11   12

Practice: counting 1–12

VALUES

8 Is Sue safe? Tick ✓. Colour and say.

Stay safe!

Values: Stay safe.

UNIT 2 REVIEW

1 Draw your favourite place at school. Colour and say.

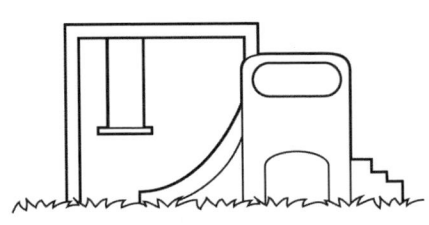

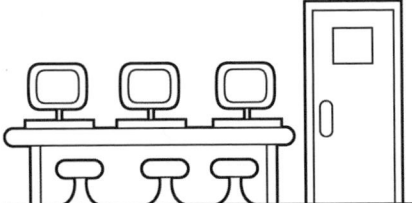

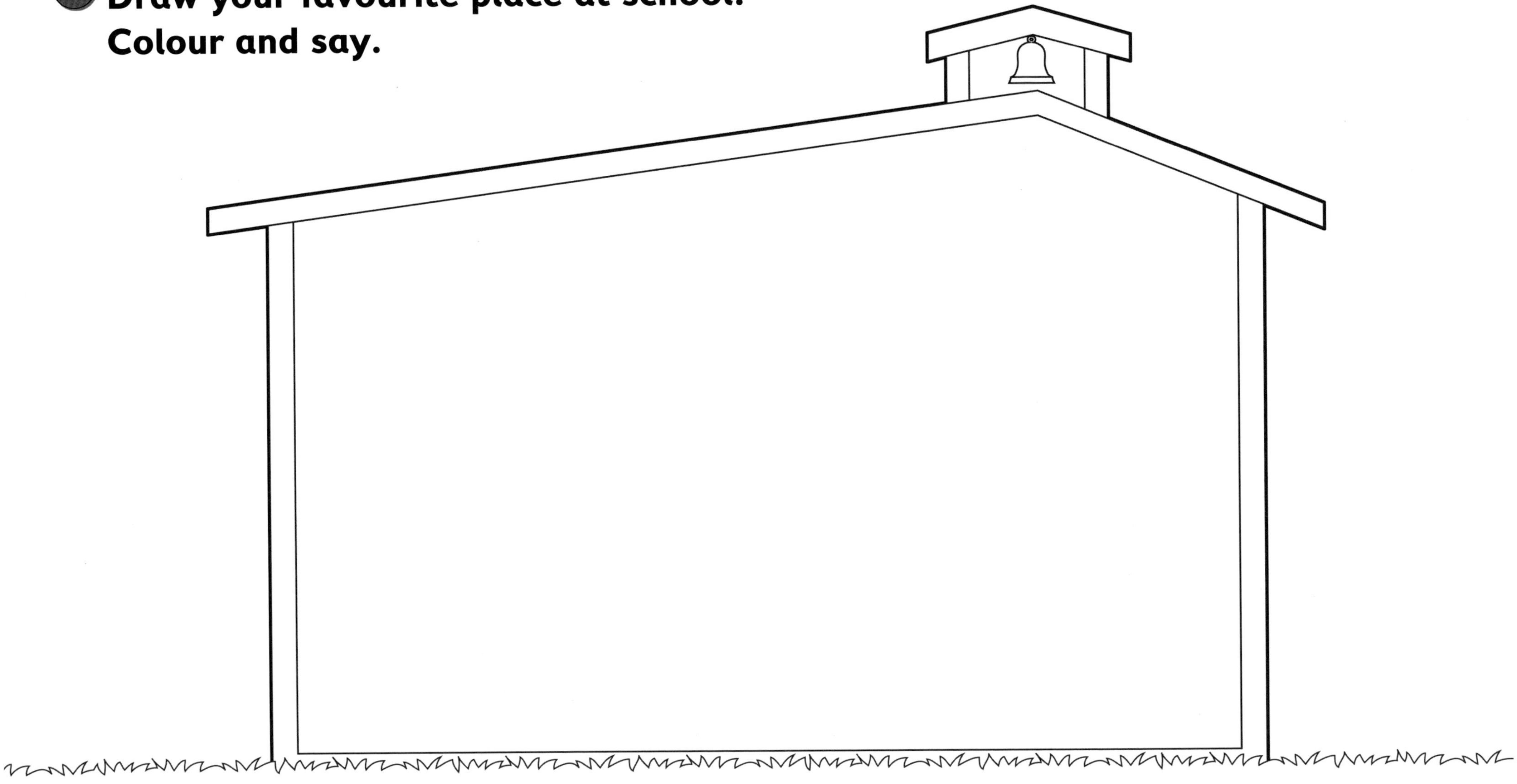

Review: *Where do you (play)? In the (playground).*

UNIT 3 REVIEW

2 Draw what you want to be. Colour and say.

Review: *What do you want to be? I want to be a (vet).*

4 My Town

1 Trace, colour, and say.

Practice: *police station* Review: *car*

VOCABULARY

2 Follow the roads. Colour and say.

Where are they going?

UNIT 4

Practice: *bus, post office, school, shop, taxi*

STORY PRACTICE

3 **Match and colour. Ask and answer.**

"Where does she work?"

Practice: *Where does (she) work? (She) works at a (hospital).*

SPEAKING

5 **Where does he/she work? Colour and say.**

Practice: *Where does (she) work? (She) works at the (police station).*

SPEAKING

6 Circle the differences in Picture B. Colour and say.

A

B

Practice: *Where does (he) work? (He) works at the (fire station).*

UNIT 4

CLIL

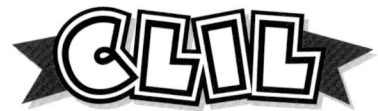

7 **Trace. Count the windows. Write and colour.**

13 14

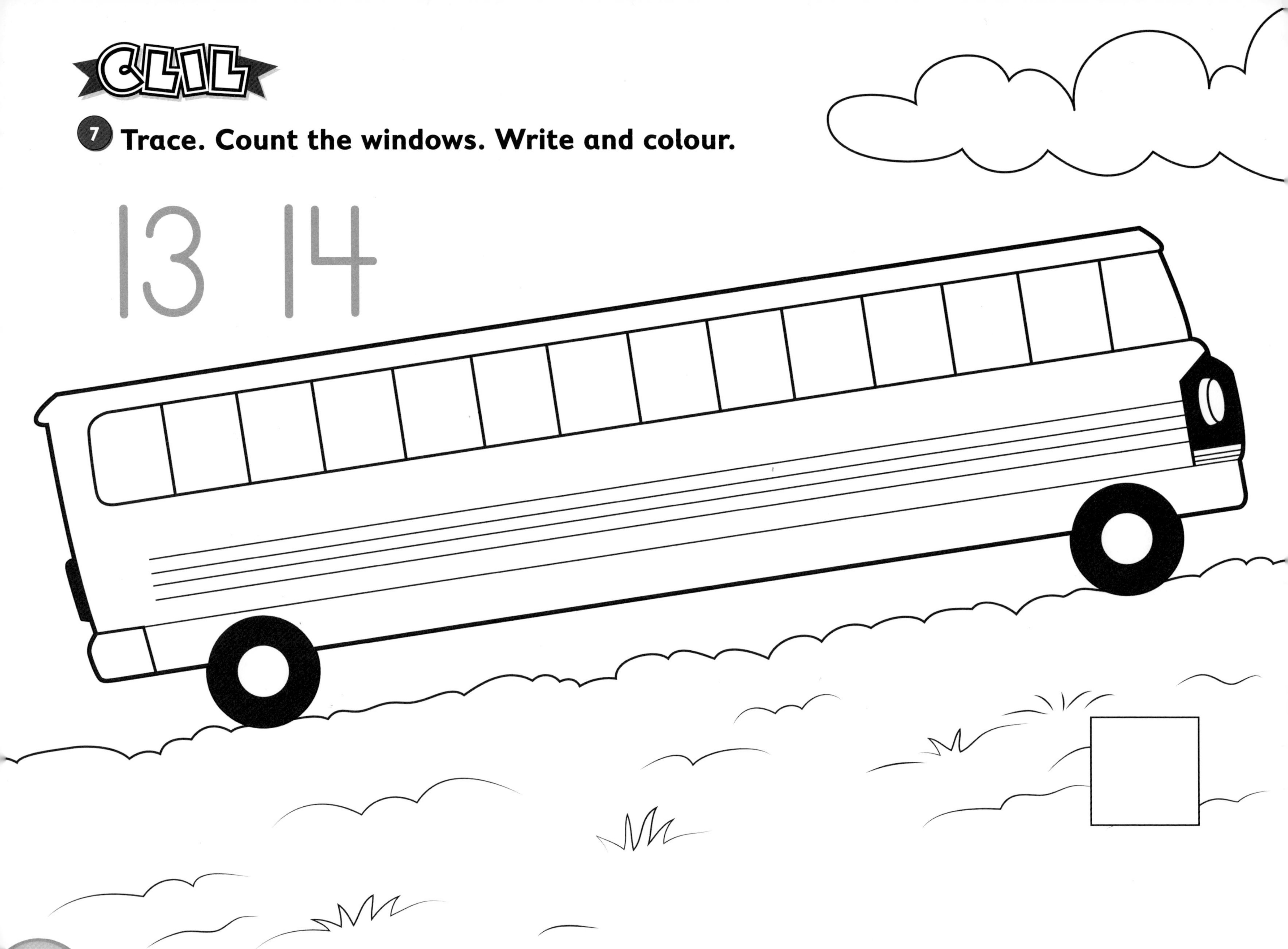

VALUES

8 Colour and say.

Ask for help.

Values: Ask for help.

5 Clothes

1 Match, colour, and say.

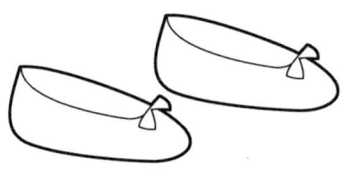
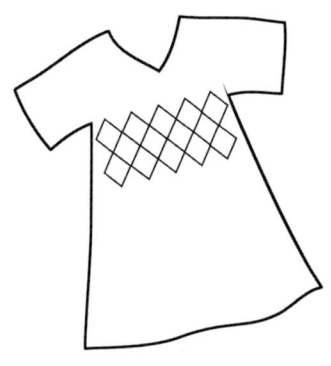

Practice: *dress, jacket, shirt, shoes, trousers*

VOCABULARY

2 **Find and colour Lou's clothes. Say.**

Practice: *shirt, shoes, socks, sweater, trousers*

UNIT 5

STORY PRACTICE

3 Circle the clothes Grandpa needs. Colour and say.

Practice: *What is (Grandpa) wearing? (He's) wearing a (shirt) and (trousers).*

5 Colour. Ask and answer.

Practice: *What's (Sue) wearing? (She's) wearing a (blue dress).*

SPEAKING

6 Trace, colour, and say.

Practice: *What's (Lou) wearing? (He's) wearing a (yellow shirt).*

UNIT 5

7 **Trace. Count the stripes. Write and colour.**

15 16

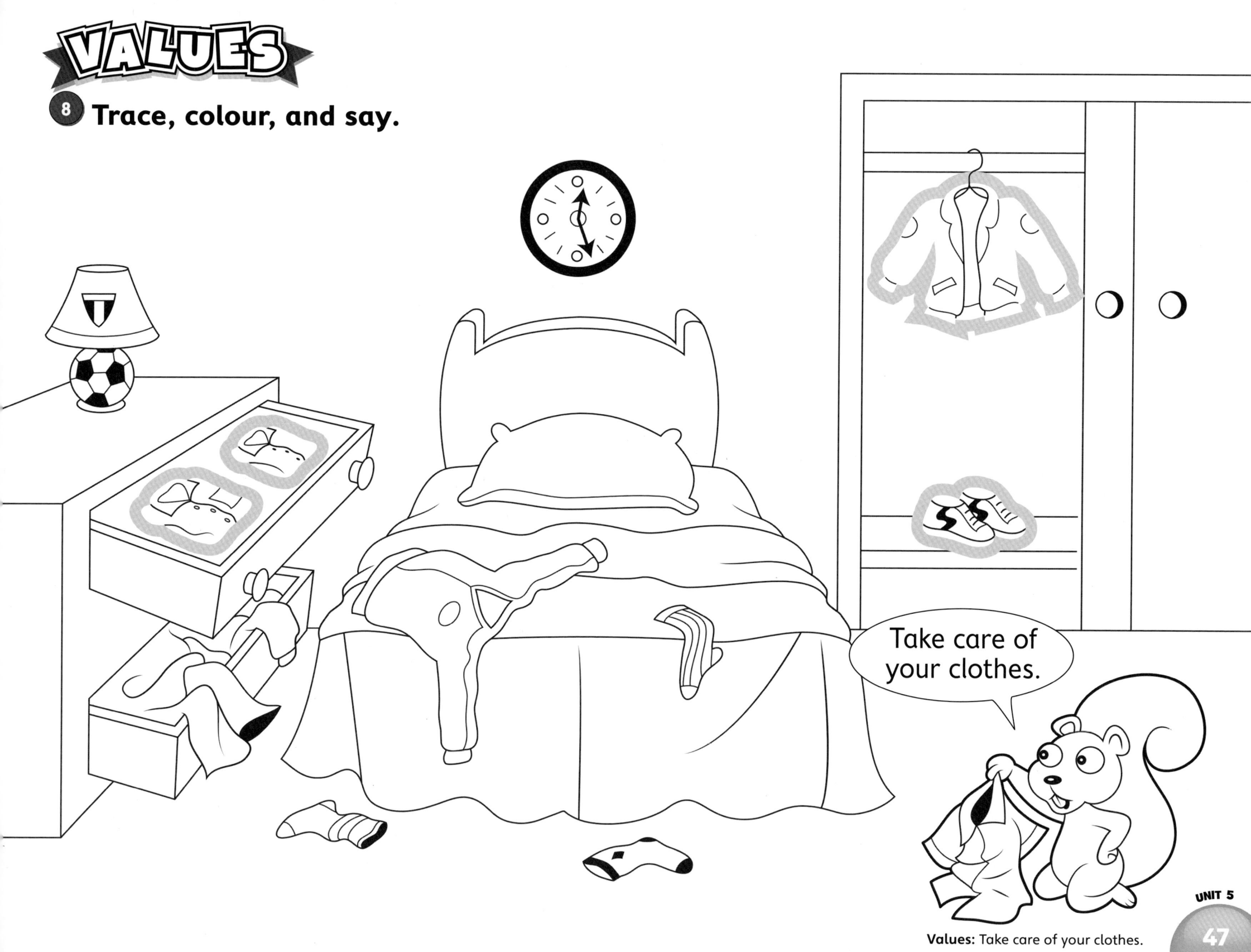

UNIT 4 REVIEW

1 Draw, colour, and say.

Where does he work?

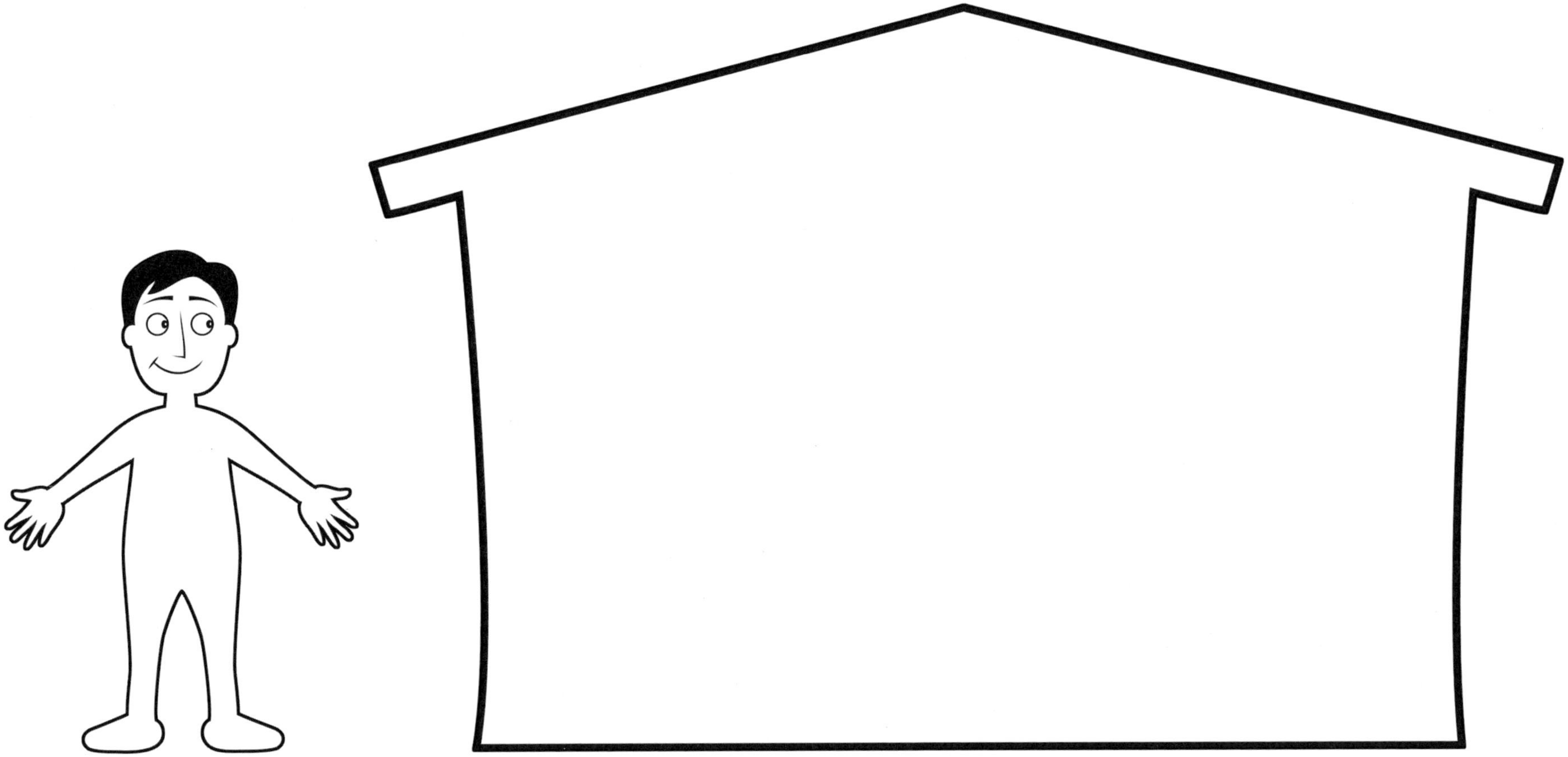

Review: *Where does (he) work? (He) works at the (school).*

UNIT 5 REVIEW

2 Draw your clothes. Colour and say.

Review: *I'm wearing a (sweater) and (trousers).*

6 Feelings

1 Draw happy or sad. Colour and say.

Happy or sad?

Practice: *happy, sad*

VOCABULARY

2 Match, colour, and say.

Practice: *sad, scared, thirsty, tired*

UNIT 6
51

STORY PRACTICE

3 Look and number. Ask and answer. Colour.

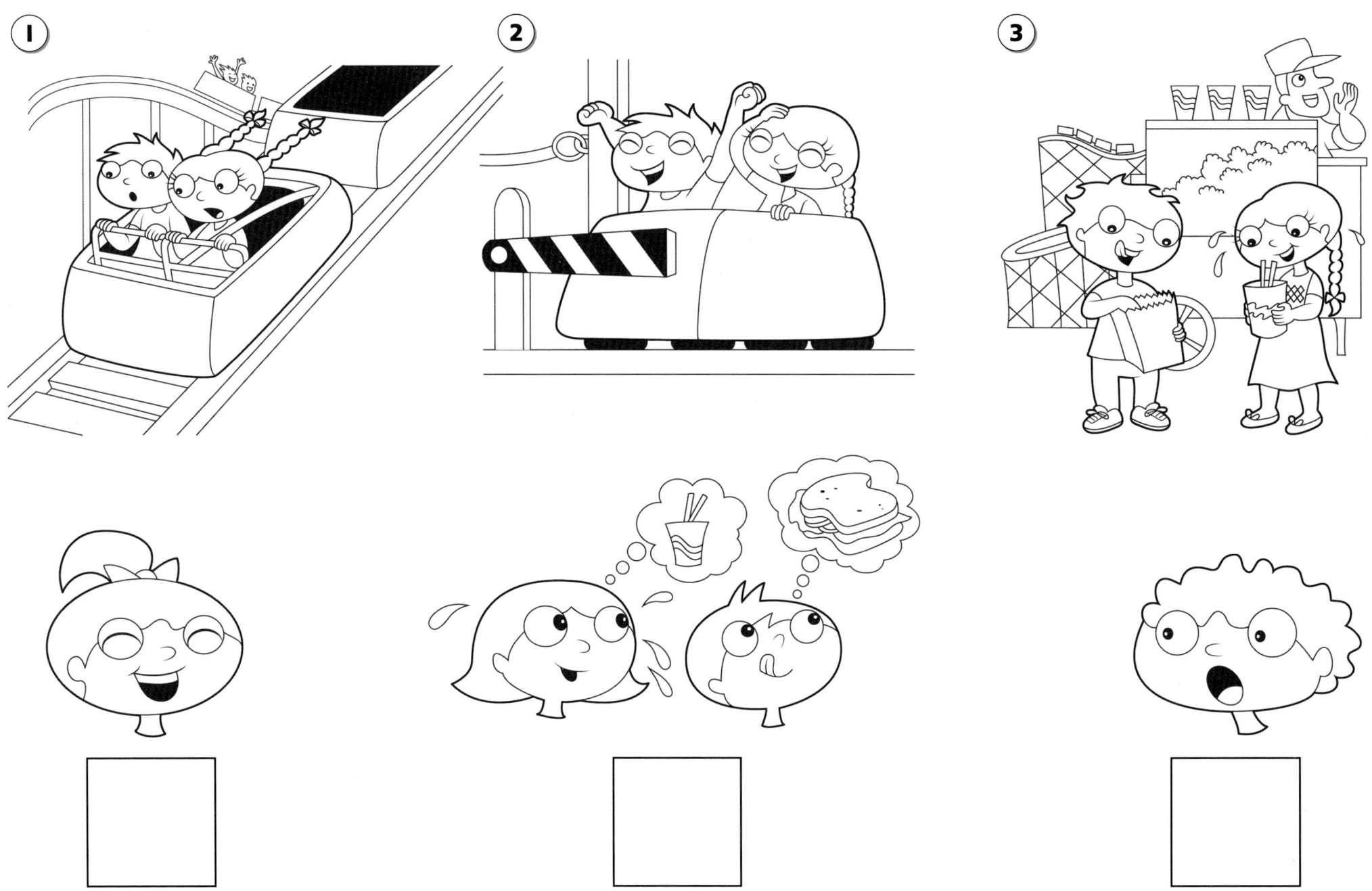

Practice: *How do you feel? I'm (scared).*

STORY PRACTICE

4 How do Sue and Lou feel in the story? Tick ✓, colour, and say.

Practice: *How do (Sue and Lou) feel? (They're) (excited).*

SPEAKING

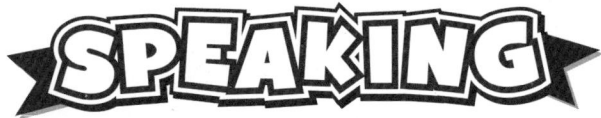

5 Draw how they feel. Ask and answer. Colour.

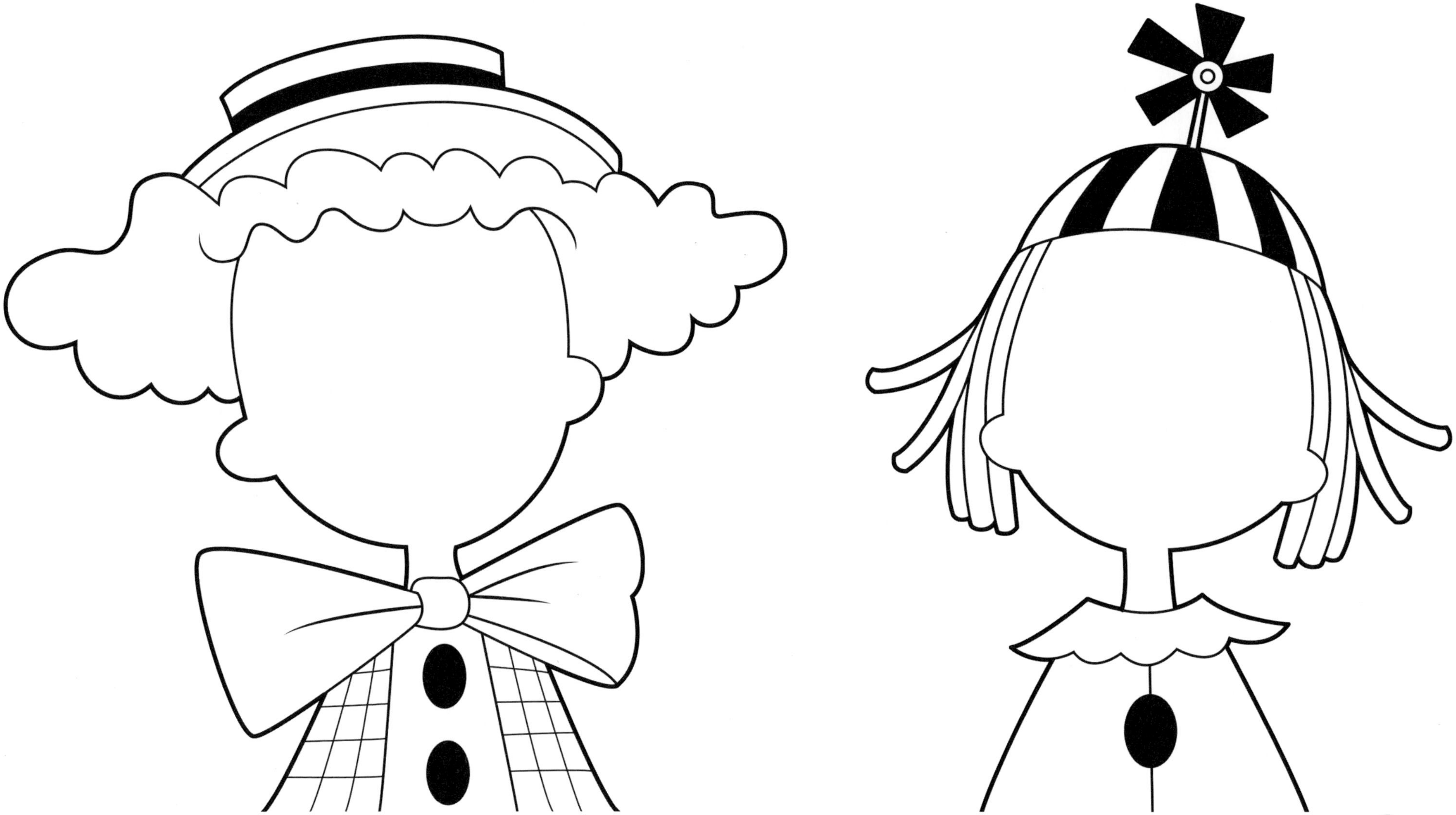

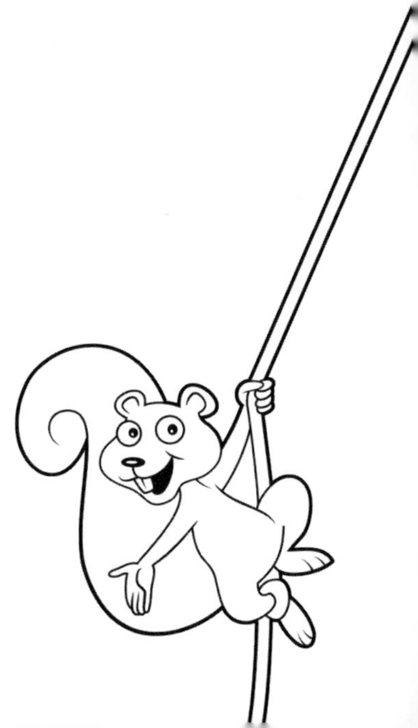

Practice: *How does (he) feel? (He's) (happy).*

SPEAKING

6 Ask and answer. Match and colour.

Practice: *How does (she) feel? (She's) (thirsty).*

UNIT 6

7 Trace, count, and write. Colour and say.   15 16 17 18

VALUES

8 **Colour and say.**

Values: Don't fight.

7 Healthy Food

1 Join the dots. Match, colour, and say.

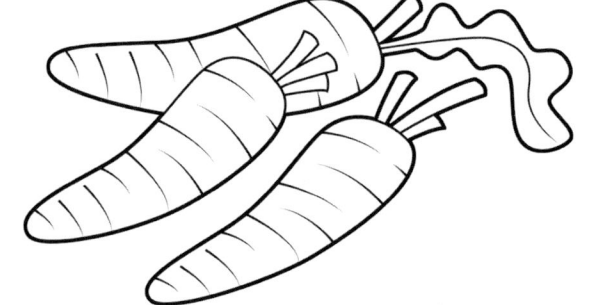

58 **Practice:** *banana, carrot, tomato* **Review:** *salad*

VOCABULARY

2 Draw, colour, and say.

Practice: *banana, carrot, lettuce, fork, mango, orange, plate, tomato*

UNIT 7

59

STORY PRACTICE

3 What does Lou want in the story? Trace the paths. Colour and say.

What do you want, Lou?

Practice: *What do you want, (Lou)? I want (an orange), please.*

STORY PRACTICE

4 What does Sue want? Circle, colour, and say.

Practice: *What do you want, (Sue)? I want (two carrots), please.*

UNIT 7

61

5 Ask and answer. Match, colour, and say.

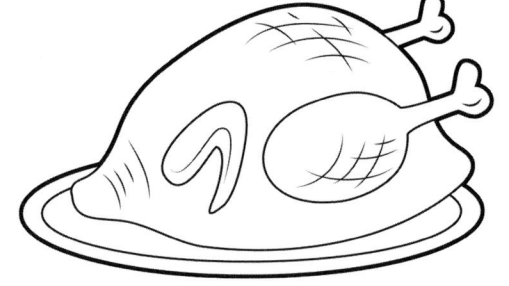

Practice: *What do you want, (Dad)? I want (chicken), please.*

SPEAKING

6 Ask and answer. Tick ✓. Colour

Practice: *What do you want? I want (an orange), please.*

UNIT 7

7 Trace. Count and write. Colour and say.   17 18 19 20

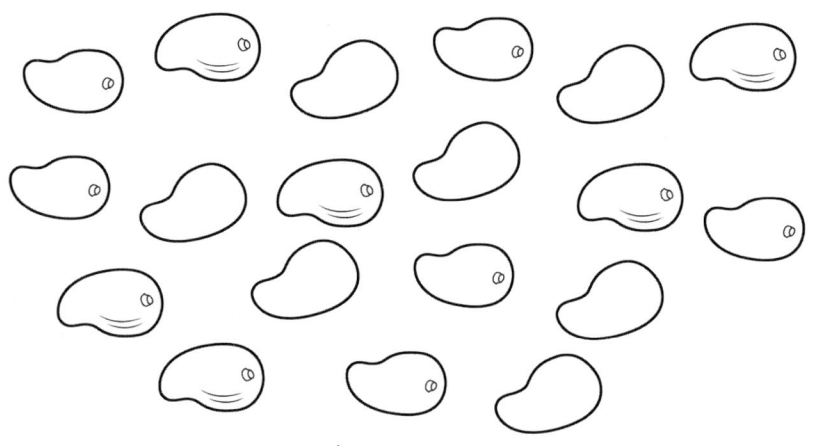

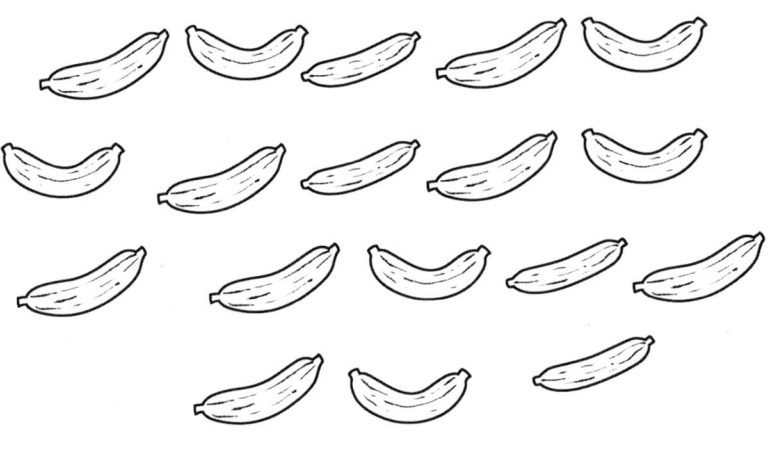

Practice: counting 1–20

UNIT 6 REVIEW

1 Draw how you feel. Colour and say.

Review: *How do you feel? I'm (tired).*

UNIT 7 REVIEW

"What do you want?"

2 Draw, colour, and say.

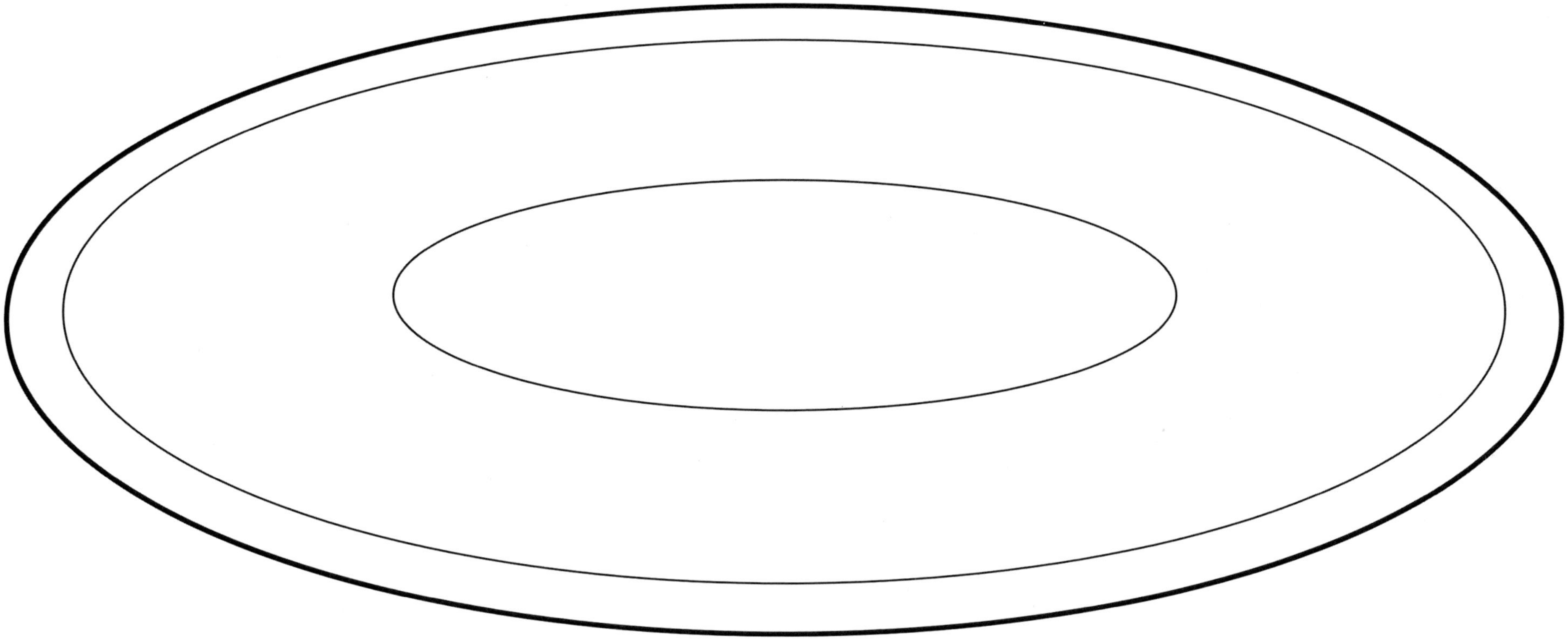

Review: *I want (a banana), please.*

8 The Zoo

1 Match, colour, and say.

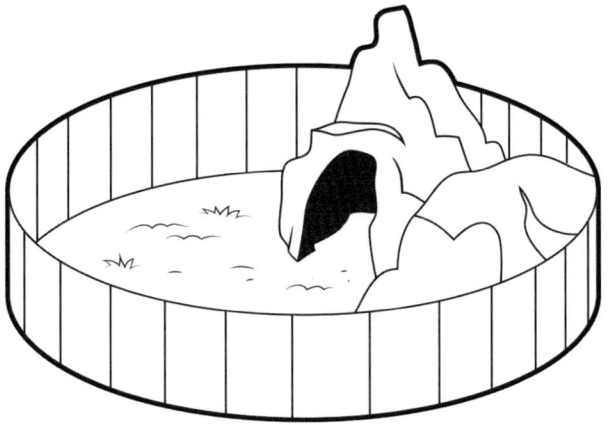

Practice: *bear, monkey, penguin*

VOCABULARY

2 What's missing? Draw, colour, and say.

Practice: *bat, elephant, lion, zebra*

UNIT 8

STORY PRACTICE

3 Circle the animals Lou and Sue see in the story. Colour and say.

Practice: *What's that? It's a (big) (elephant).*

STORY PRACTICE

4 Trace and match. Colour and say.

"What's that?"

1

2

3

Practice: *What's that? It's a (small) (bat).*

SPEAKING

5 Colour the big lion. Ask and answer.

Practice: *What's that? It's a (big) (lion).*

SPEAKING

6 Ask and answer. Colour.

Practice: *What's that? It's a (big) (zebra).*

7 Trace. Add and draw.

Practice: simple addition

9 Places

1 Trace, colour, and say.

Practice: *building, mountain, river, traffic light*

VOCABULARY

2 Match, colour, and say.

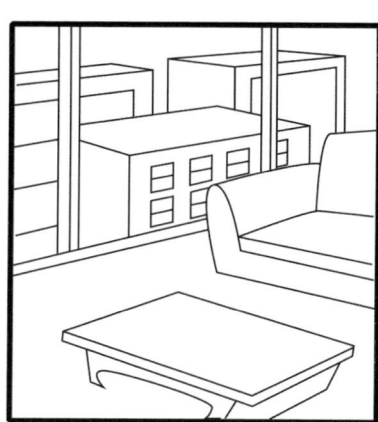
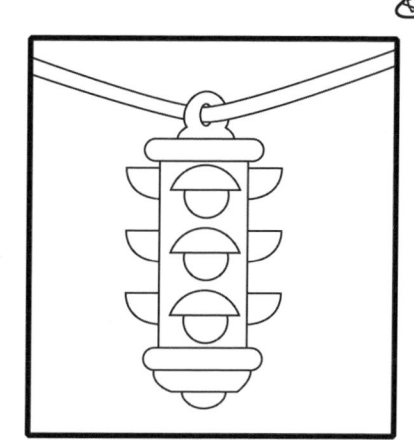

Practice: building, field, flat, forest, mountain, river, street, traffic light

UNIT 9

77

4 Join the dots. Colour and say.

Practice: (Bears) live in the (city), too.

SPEAKING

5 Match. Ask and answer. Colour.

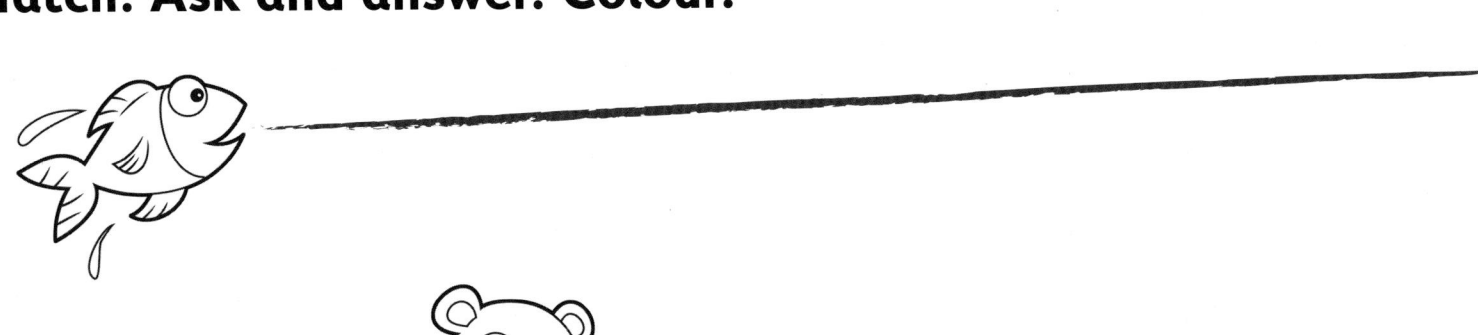

Practice: *Where do (fish) live? (They) live in the (river).*

SPEAKING

6 Trace the paths. Ask and answer. Colour.

Practice: *Where does (the duck) live? (It) lives in the (river).*

7 Trace. Take away and draw.   1 2 3 4 5

Practice: simple taking away   Review: *apples, cows, ducks, trees*

UNIT 8 REVIEW

1 Draw your favourite animal. Colour and say.

Review: *It's a (big) (bear).*

UNIT 9 REVIEW

2 **Where do you live? Draw, colour, and say.**

Where do you live?

    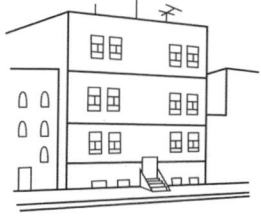 

Review: *(I) live in the (city).*

UNIT 2 PHONICS

Colour, trace and say.

 cat

 hen

 jump

Phonics: initial c, h, j Review: *cat, hen, jump*

UNIT 3

Colour, trace and say.

queen

red

vet

Phonics: initial *q, r, v* **Review:** *red, vet*

UNIT 4  PHONICS

Colour, trace and say.

windy

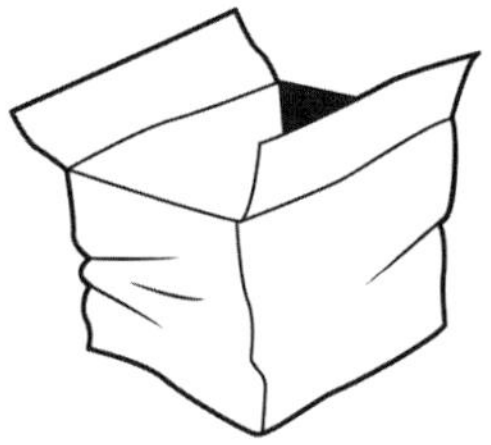

box

yoghurt

Practice: initial *w*, *y*, and final *x* **Review:** *box, windy, yogurt*

UNIT 5 PHONICS

Colour, trace and say.

e

b d 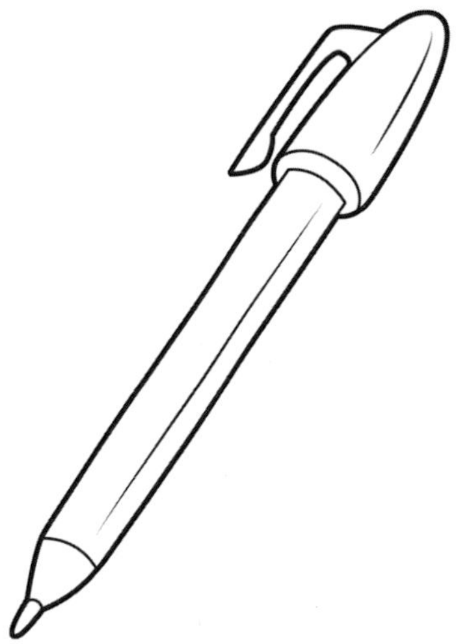   p n    h n

Phonics: short e Review: *bed, hen, pen*

89

UNIT 6 PHONICS

Colour, trace and say.

c _ t

_ d d

h _ nd

Phonics: short *a* Review: *cat, dad, hand*

UNIT 7 PHONICS

Colour, trace and say.

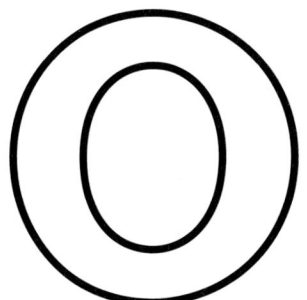

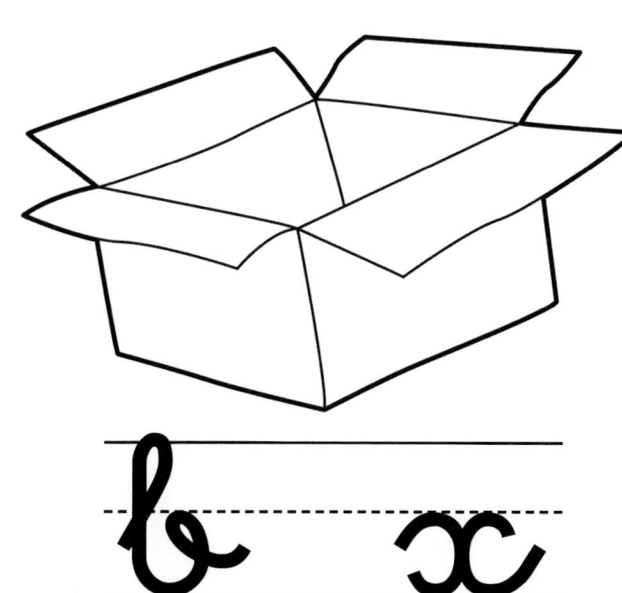

h _ t   d _ ll   b _ x

Phonics: short o **Review:** *box, doll, hot*

UNIT 8 PHONICS

Colour, trace and say.

s _ n

c _ p

b _ s

Phonics: short *u* Review: *bus, cup, sun*

UNIT 9 PHONICS

Colour, trace and say.

i

s_t   f_sh   m_lk

Phonics: short *i* **Review:** *fish, milk, sit*

Congratulations!

_____

has finished Activity Book 3.

CUTOUTS

Cut out one or more for page 94.

95

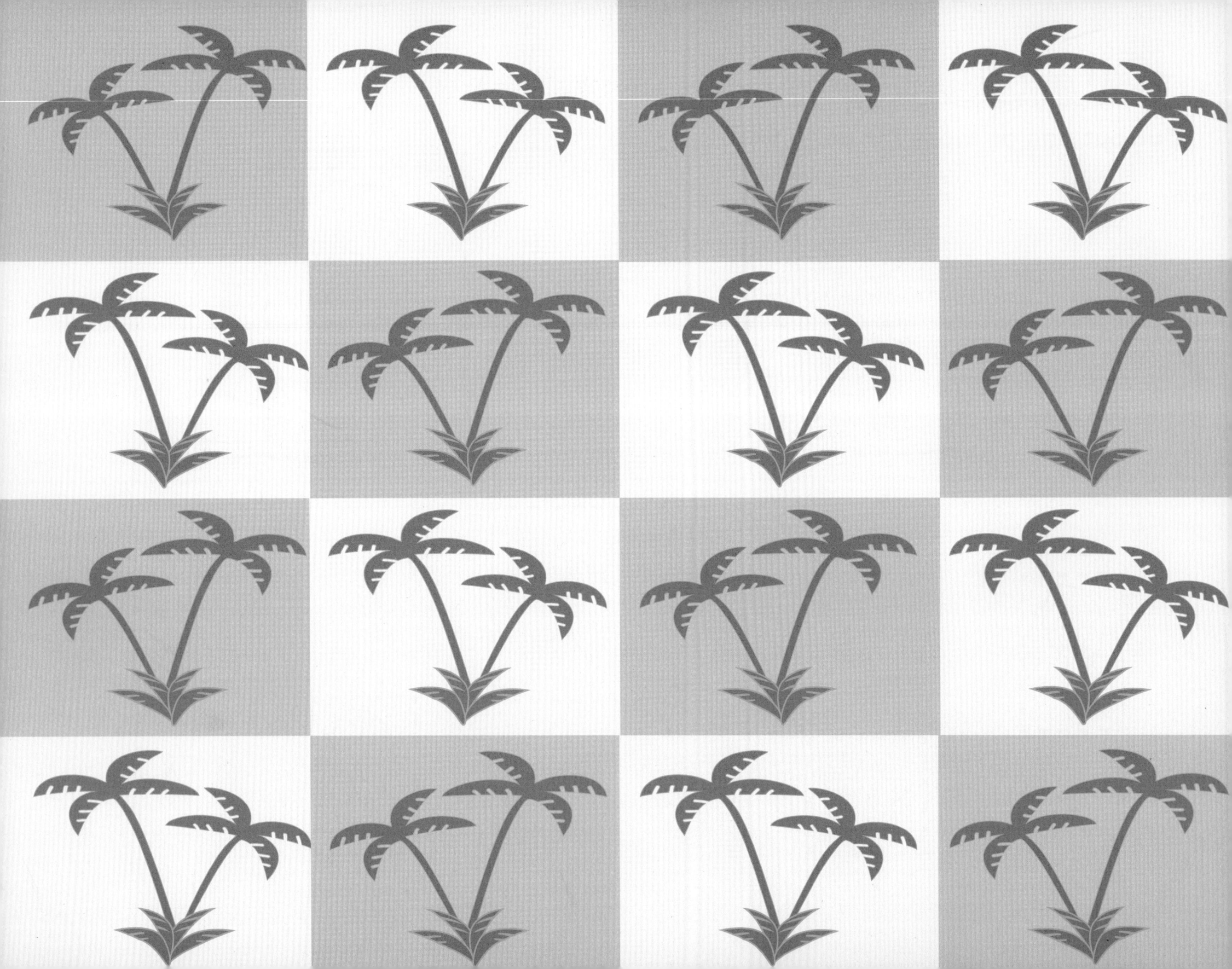